REBECCA LAFFAR-SMITH

PLOT STORMING

Your Book Title
_____

by

Your Author Name
_____

A Novel Writer's Workbook
Define Story Structure
The Hero's Journey, and
Character Development

Welcome to a new adventure into creative discovery and structure!

I'm so delighted you've decided to pick up this workbook.
It's not much, because it's not the true teaching tool.
Let me tell you why!

This workbook is your place to brainstorm, to create, to play and flex.
It's a place to flesh out your ideas and a place to make mistakes.
In this workbook you can scratch out and scrawl and explore.

There's no wrong way to use the workbook,
but you might not find it truly useful on its own
because it's designed to be a tool in support of something bigger.
This tool is designed to go with my **Plot Storming Workshop**.

The great thing is, along with this workbook, you also
get free access to the online version of my workshop in webinar form.

Access the free webinar here:
http://www.rebeccalaffarsmith.com/plot-storming-webinar/

And if you have any questions, want some support or brainstorming
assistance, need extra help to understand any aspects of
what I cover in the workshop, or just want a new writing buddy.

Feel free to email me! admin@rebeccalaffarsmith.com

PART
ONE

Finding Your Sweetspot
and Defining Your Novel

The Planner vs Pantser Quiz

1. You get the idea for a character while washing dishes one evening.
   a) You immediately dry your hands, take note of every detail, branch off, brainstorm and freewrite to explore all the possible characteristics and potential stories this character could be involved in.
   b) You dry your hands and swiftly note down significant key points as memory joggers then return to the suds.
   c) You continue to ponder the character as you wash, rinse, and dry then write down your final findings and concepts.
   d) You think it over but continue with the dishes and decide to write about it at some unspecified time in the future.
   e) You go off (either immediately or after the dishes) and begin a brand new story with this character as the star.

2. You're asked to write a play for the Pre-Ks at the local community center.
   a) You stare at a blank page for a few hours (or days) then right before the deadline rush together a few pages the kids will have fun with.
   b) You go to the center, talk to the kids and teachers to get an idea of their interests, abilities, and individual characters.
   c) You head straight home and pull out a dusty script about your pet dog that you wrote in grade school.
   d) You craft an outline and consider the various roles and the ramifications of a moral theme.
   e) You scratch out the first page of a dozen ideas but can't settle on just one for the kids play.

3. You've just finished reading the final installment of a fantastically detailed trilogy.
   a) You are still ga-ga over the characters and the intricacy of the plot and have been totally swept away by the story.
   b) You allow your mind to play connect-the-dots with the plot and enjoy the intricate and careful crafting involved.
   c) You start experimenting with fan-fiction off-shoots because you're hooked on the characters and want more adventures for them.
   d) You gape at the astounding beauty of the piece and give up writing because you "know" you couldn't possibly match it.
   e) You start reading the books again; making notes in the margins and underlining notable passages, dissecting the book to see how the author accomplished it.

4. Your midway through writing chapter five when you decide you really can't stand your protagonist.
   a) You stop writing immediately, shelve the manuscript, and decide you'll come back "someday" when you understand her better.
   b) You stop writing and start examining your mood, the more recent events, and the character to first determine why you no longer like him and then how to "fix" him.
   c) You keep writing and decide to see where she's headed before you act.
   d) You keep writing but add a dramatic death scene within the next couple of pages turning your focus on a new or secondary character instead.
   e) You spend a short time giving your character an interview to discuss her thoughts and see if you can work out, together, what to do next.

5. A new family move next door and you hear strange noises at night but see nothing of them during the day.
   a) You call the police to report the weirdos but later discover that the mother is simply a shift worker, the father's a novelist, and the oldest child is a rap-loving teenager.
   b) You watch from your upstairs office window, trying to see their vampire teeth or wolves fur in the moonlight.
   c) You start playing the "what if" game and generate some great story ideas based on what this family could be if they were characters in a book.
   d) You start writing blog entries or shorts about them, each with a wilder explanation than the last.
   e) You go over, introduce yourself, offer a cup of sugar and hear all about their recent trip to Brazil and her obsession with photography – all fodder for your next book.

Tally Your Points:
1) a. 5, b. 4, c. 3, d. 2, e. 1
2) a. 3, b. 5, c. 2, d. 4, e. 1
3) a. 3, b. 4, c. 1, d. 2, e. 5
4) a. 3, b. 5, c. 1, d. 2, e. 4
5) a. 3, b. 2, c. 4, d. 1, e. 5

Your Result

5 – 7 points [Pantser]
You're a true Pantser. You can fly with any idea and love to leap before you look. You've got pages of stories started but rarely finished and love to play around with new concepts, tying it all together with creativity and an exciting flare for adventure.

8 – 12 points [Pre-Pantser]
You'd love to throw caution to the winds but often hold back from just diving right in. You prefer to consider multiple options but can go along with any challenge and turn any good idea into a potential story.

13 – 17 points [Middle Grounder]
You're in the safe zone and often struggle to write anything at all. You enjoy exploring ideas but want to find the best ones and don't like wasting time writing about things you aren't passionate about. You'll start stories with some planning but also enjoy the adventure of taking detours.

18 – 22 points [Pre-Planner]
You like to do the legwork in your mind. You'll sometimes plan things out and often have the basic map laid out in your head but keep adding to your plans and are flexible for changes. You generally have a solid destination in mind when you begin writing but aren't sure of all the roads you'll need to take to get their. You're familiar with your main characters but often face blocks caused by being unsure what course they would most likely take in a given situation.

23 – 25 points [Planner]
You like to brainstorm and outline every detail before you begin. You know your characters intimately and understand their deep motivations. You can be a little pedantic and often spend so much time planning and researching that you don't leave enough to actually spend writing. When you do write you know exactly what to expect from every scene and work intricate details across our novel like knitting a sweater.

[Disclaimer: This quiz is mearly a quick, fun way to get a sense of where you stand on the planner/pantser spectrum. Is not scientific and results may vary.]

Your Sweet Spot Map

I LOVE...

I HATE...

I NEED...

Date: _____

I FEAR...

I AM
DRAWN TO...

I GET
SHIVERS
FROM...

Notes:

List of Categories/Genres

Biographies & Memoirs
Humour & Entertainment

Literature & Fiction
    Action & Adventure
    Ancient & Medieval
    Mythology & Folk Tales
    Women's Fiction

Mystery, Thriller & Suspense
    Mystery
        British Detectives
        Cozy
        Hard-Boiled
        Police Procedurals
        Supernatural
        Women Sleuths
    Thriller & Suspense
        Crime
        Legal
        Medical
        Military
        Psychological Thrillers
        Spies & Politics
        Supernatural
        Technothrillers

Romance
    Contemporary
    Erotica
    Fantasy
    Gay Romance
    Gothic
    Lesbian Romance
    Military
    Paranormal
    Regency
    Romantic Comedy
    Romantic Suspense
    Science Fiction
    Time Travel
    Vampires
    Western

Science Fiction & Fantasy
    Fantasy
        Alternate History
        Dark
        Epic
        Paranormal & Urban
        Superheroes
        Sword & Sorcery
    Science Fiction
        Adventure
        Alien Invasion
        Alternate History
        Dystopian
        High Tech
        Military
        Post-Apocalyptic
        Space Opera
        Steampunk
        Time Travel

Teen & Young Adult
    Historical Fiction
    Horror
    Love & Romance
    Mysteries
    Science Fiction & Fantasy

Most genres also have a Historical sub-category.

This is just a short list of some of the hottest categories available on Amazon. Other booksellers and book reviewing websites will have other categories. It's important to do some research into categories and genre so that you have an idea of what is available and what the normal tendencies (tropes) for those genres are. If you write mysteries, for example, you will need to know the difference between a Cozy and a Police Procedural. To create a book that has market potential you need to understand it's place in the market and write within those market conventions.

Remember the structure of a Story Sentence / Elevator Pitch:

Protagonist - Antagonist - Conflict - Setting - Twist

Two words to describe the protagonist
Two words to describe the antagonist
The key element of their conflict
The tone of the story setting
and an element of twist.

Notes:

_____   _____
_____   _____
_____   _____
_____   _____
_____   _____
_____   _____
_____   _____
_____   _____
_____   _____
_____   _____
_____   _____
_____   _____
_____   _____
_____   _____
_____   _____
_____   _____
_____   _____
_____   _____

Define Your Novel

Working Title: _____

Genre: 1. _____

            2. _____

Reader Age: _____

Target Length: _____

Core Theme or Message:

_____

_____

Story Sentence / Elevator Pitch:

_____

_____

_____

_____

_____

_____

_____

_____

_____

Brainstorm Your Ideas:

Explore Your Ideas:

PART
TWO

**Character Archetypes and
Casting Your Characters**

Notes:

Cast of Characters

HERO: _____

SHADOW: _____

MENTOR: _____

THRESHOLD
GUARDIANS: _____
_____
_____

HERALD/S: _____
_____
_____

SHIFTER/S: _____
_____
_____

TRICKSTER/S: _____
_____
_____

Character
Sketch

Role in Story: _____ Hero (Protagonist) _____

Goal: _____

Ambition: _____

Motivation: _____

Values:

1. Nothing is more important than

_____

2. Nothing is more important than

_____

3. Nothing is more important than

_____

Fatal Flaw: _____

Conflict: _____

Epiphany: _____

Sentence: _____

_____

Paragraph:

_____

_____

_____

Character Background:

_____

_____

– _____

_____

_____

Habits & Mannerisms:

_____

_____

PHYSICAL APPEARANCE

Birthdate: _____

Age: _____

Height: _____

Weight: _____

Ethnicity: _____

Style of dress: _____

Hair & Eyes: _____

Physical Description:

_____

_____

_____

PERSONALITY

Personality Type: _____

Sense of Humour: _____

Religion: _____

Politics: _____

Hobbies: _____

Favourite Colour: _____

Favourite Music: _____

Favourite Books: _____

Favourite Movies: _____

Contents of Bag: _____

ENVIRONMENT

Occupation: _____

Education: _____

Description of Home: _____

_____

Family: _____

_____

Best Friend: _____

Male Friends: _____

Female Friends: _____

Enemies: _____

PSYCHOLOGICAL

Best Childhood Memory: _____

Worst Childhood Memory: _____

One-Line Characterisation: _____

Strongest Character Traits: _____

Weakest Character Traits: _____

Character's Paradox: _____

_____

Greatest Hope: _____

Greatest Fear: _____

How He/She See's Self: _____

How Others See Him/Her: _____

Life Philosophy: _____

_____

Notes:

_____

_____

_____

_____

Notes:

Character
Sketch

Role in Story: _____ Shadow (Antagonist) _____

Goal: _____

Ambition: _____

Motivation: _____

Values:

1. Nothing is more important than

_____

2. Nothing is more important than

_____

3. Nothing is more important than

_____

Fatal Flaw: _____

Conflict: _____

Epiphany: _____

Sentence: _____

_____

Paragraph: _____

_____

_____

_____

Character Background:

_____

_____

_ _____

_____

_____

Habits & Mannerisms:

_____

_____

PHYSICAL APPEARANCE

Birthdate: _____

Age: _____

Height: _____

Weight: _____

Ethnicity: _____

Style of dress: _____

Hair & Eyes: _____

Physical Description:

_____

_____

_____

PERSONALITY

Personality Type: _____

Sense of Humour: _____

Religion: _____

Politics: _____

Hobbies: _____

Favourite Colour: _____

Favourite Music: _____

Favourite Books: _____

Favourite Movies: _____

Contents of Bag: _____

ENVIRONMENT

Occupation: _____

Education: _____

Description of Home: _____

_____

Family: _____

_____

Best Friend: _____

Male Friends: _____

Female Friends: _____

Enemies: _____ 27

PSYCHOLOGICAL

Best Childhood Memory: _____

Worst Childhood Memory: _____

One-Line Characterisation: _____

Strongest Character Traits: _____

Weakest Character Traits: _____

Character's Paradox: _____

_____

Greatest Hope: _____

Greatest Fear: _____

How He/She See's Self: _____

How Others See Him/Her: _____

Life Philosophy: _____

_____

Notes:

_____

_____

_____

_____

Notes:

Character
Sketch

Role in Story: _____

Goal: _____

Ambition: _____

Motivation: _____

Values:

1. Nothing is more important than

_____

2. Nothing is more important than

_____

3. Nothing is more important than

_____

Fatal Flaw: _____

Conflict: _____

Epiphany: _____

Sentence: _____

_____

Paragraph: _____

_____

_____

_____

Character Background:

_____

_____

_ _____

_____

_____

Habits & Mannerisms:

_____

_____

PHYSICAL APPEARANCE

Birthdate: _____

Age: _____

Height: _____

Weight: _____

Ethnicity: _____

Style of dress: _____

Hair & Eyes: _____

Physical Description:

_____

_____

_____

PERSONALITY

Personality Type: _____

Sense of Humour: _____

Religion: _____

Politics: _____

Hobbies: _____

Favourite Colour: _____

Favourite Music: _____

Favourite Books: _____

Favourite Movies: _____

Contents of Bag: _____

ENVIRONMENT

Occupation: _____

Education: _____

Description of Home: _____

_____

Family: _____

_____

Best Friend: _____

Male Friends: _____

Female Friends: _____

Enemies: _____

PSYCHOLOGICAL

Best Childhood Memory: _____

Worst Childhood Memory: _____

One-Line Characterisation: _____

Strongest Character Traits: _____

Weakest Character Traits: _____

Character's Paradox: _____

_____

Greatest Hope: _____

Greatest Fear: _____

How He/She See's Self: _____

How Others See Him/Her: _____

Life Philosophy: _____

_____

Notes:

_____

_____

_____

_____

_____

Notes:

Character
Sketch

Character Name

Role in Story: _____

Goal: _____

Ambition: _____

Motivation: _____

Values:

1. Nothing is more important than

_____

2. Nothing is more important than

_____

3. Nothing is more important than

_____

Fatal Flaw: _____

Conflict: _____

Epiphany: _____

Sentence: _____

_____

Paragraph: _____

_____

_____

_____

Character Background:

_____

_____

__ _____

_____

_____

Habits & Mannerisms:

_____

_____

PHYSICAL APPEARANCE

Birthdate: _____

Age: _____

Height: _____

Weight: _____

Ethnicity: _____

Style of dress: _____

Hair & Eyes: _____

Physical Description:

_____

_____

_____

PERSONALITY

Personality Type: _____

Sense of Humour: _____

Religion: _____

Politics: _____

Hobbies: _____

Favourite Colour: _____

Favourite Music: _____

Favourite Books: _____

Favourite Movies: _____

Contents of Bag: _____

ENVIRONMENT

Occupation: _____

Education: _____

Description of Home: _____

_____

Family: _____

_____

Best Friend: _____

Male Friends: _____

Female Friends: _____

Enemies: _____

PSYCHOLOGICAL

Best Childhood Memory: _____

Worst Childhood Memory: _____

One-Line Characterisation: _____

Strongest Character Traits: _____

Weakest Character Traits: _____

Character's Paradox: _____

_____

Greatest Hope: _____

Greatest Fear: _____

How He/She See's Self: _____

How Others See Him/Her: _____

Life Philosophy: _____

_____

Notes:

_____

_____

_____

_____

_____

Notes:

42

Setting Sketches

STORY SETTINGS

PART
THREE

The Hero's Journey
Act I

The Hero's Journey Broken Down

Ordinary World: This portrays the normal, ordinary life of the Hero. Some genres have a scene prior this that foreshadows the inciting incident.

Call To Adventure: Something happens that upsets the Hero's status quo.

Refusal of the Call: The Hero, reluctant to change, resists taking action.

Notes:

_____   _____
_____   _____
_____   _____
_____   _____
_____   _____
_____   _____
_____   _____
_____   _____
_____   _____
_____   _____
_____   _____
_____   _____
_____   _____
_____   _____
_____   _____
_____   _____
_____   _____
_____   _____

Story Beats: Act I

Ordinary World / Limited Awareness:

_____
_____
_____
_____
_____
_____
_____

Call to Adventure / Inciting Incident / Increased Awareness:

_____
_____
_____
_____
_____
_____
_____

Refusal of the Call / Reluctance to Change:

_____
_____
_____
_____
_____
_____

The Hero's Journey Broken Down

Meeting The Mentor: A wise guide appears who will help the Hero grow. This Mentor gives advice, guidance, and a gentle nudge in the right direction.

Crossing The First Threshold: And so, the Hero makes a conscious choice to willingly step into the unknown. Threshold crossings show movement and transition from one place to another. These are often fast-paced scenes.

Notes:

Story Beats: Act I

Meeting with the Mentor / Supernatural Aid / Overcoming:

_____

_____

_____

_____

_____

_____

_____

_____

_____

_____

Crossing the First Threshold / Committing:

_____

_____

_____

_____

_____

_____

_____

_____

_____

_____

_____

Story Beats: Act I

Meeting with the Mentor / Supernatural Aid / Overcoming:

_____
_____
_____
_____
_____
_____
_____
_____
_____
_____

Crossing the First Threshold / Committing:

_____
_____
_____
_____
_____
_____
_____
_____
_____
_____
_____

PART
FOUR

The Hero's Journey
Act II

The Hero's Journey Broken Down

Tests, Allies & Enemies: The Hero meets characters who may help or hinder his progress and present trials and challenges along the way. This may equate to several scenes.

Midpoint: A turning point from ignorance to understanding. The Hero faces a reversal and new truth. Often heralded with a vertical motion or first kiss.

Notes:

_____   _____
_____   _____
_____   _____
_____   _____
_____   _____
_____   _____
_____   _____
_____   _____
_____   _____
_____   _____
_____   _____
_____   _____
_____   _____
_____   _____
_____   _____
_____   _____
_____   _____
_____   _____
_____   _____
_____   _____
_____

Story Beats: Act II (part 1)

Tests, Allies & Enemies / The Road of Trials:

_____
_____
_____
_____
_____
_____
_____
_____
_____
_____
_____
_____
_____
_____
_____
_____
_____
_____

Midpoint / Meeting with the Goddess / Big Change:

_____
_____
_____
_____
_____
_____
_____

The Hero's Journey Broken Down

Approach to the Inmost Cave: The Hero must face his worst fears, face down a threshold guardian and overcome a character flaw before he can find success.

Death of the Mentor: Confronted by the Shadow, a sacrifice is made. The Hero is often at his most helpless. His Mentor is lost to him and he feels defeated.

Seizing the Sword: When all hope is lost, a boon or gift appears.

Notes:

Story Beats: Act II (part 2)

Approach to the Inmost Cave / Crossing the Second Threshold:

_____

_____

_____

_____

_____

_____

_____

Death of the Mentor / The Ordeal:

_____

_____

_____

_____

_____

_____

_____

Seizing the Sword / Reward / The Ultimate Boon:

_____

_____

_____

_____

_____

_____

PART
FIVE

The Hero's Journey
Act III

The Hero's Journey Broken Down

The Road Back: It's time to begin the journey back from darkness. It often invovles a chase or escape scene with vertical movement. The Hero chooses to face his greatest battle and approaches the Shadow.

Master of Two Worlds: Now the Hero must face down his enemies, and himself. He gives up his old self and accepts his new strength. Sometimes, guidance or aid comes from a resurrection of the mentor.

Return with the Elixir: The Hero returns to the ordinary world, changed and triumphant. The journey comes full circle, mirroring the story's beginning.

Notes:

Story Beats: Act III

The Road Back / Crossing the Return Threshold:

_____
_____
_____
_____
_____
_____
_____

Master of Two Worlds / Resurrection:

_____
_____
_____
_____
_____
_____
_____

Return with the Elixir / Freedom to Life:

_____
_____
_____
_____
_____

Notes:

Notes:

Notes:

Notes:

If you found this workbook useful
please take a moment to
write a review on Amazon.

Your feedback, support, and shared stories
about how this workbook has helped you
can make a big difference in helping other
writers choose the tools that will help them
in their own journey of creation.

It also means a lot to creators and writers
like me, who don't have the support of
major publishing houses and depend on our
readers and fellow writers to spread the word.

And, remember, if you'd like support in your writing journey
I'm just an email away! admin@rebeccalaffarsmith.com

You can also follow me on social media: @laffarsmith

I love meeting fellow authors and writers
and welcome you to be part of our community.

Happy Writing!

Rebecca Laffar-Smith

www.ingramcontent.com/pod-product-compliance
Lightning Source LLC
Chambersburg PA
CBHW080900030426
42334CB00021B/2614